THE DAY HOSPITAL

Sally Read was born in Suffolk in 1971. She trained and worked as a psychiatric nurse in London while completing a BA with the Open University, and went on to earn her MA at the University of South Dakota, USA. She received an Eric Gregory Award in 2001. Her three poetry collections with Bloodaxe are: *The Point of Splitting* (2005), which was shortlisted for the Jerwood-Aldeburgh First Collection Prize, *Broken Sleep* (2009) and *The Day Hospital* (2012). The Poetry Archive released her audio CD, *Sally Read reading from her poems*, in 2010.

Her poems have appeared in several anthologies, including Roddy Lumsden's *Identity Parade* (Bloodaxe Books, 2010), *The Picador Book of Love Poems* (2011) and *Poems of the Decade* (Forward Publishing, 2011). A selected poems in Italian, translated by Andrea Sirotti and Loredana Magazzeni, is nearing completion. She is a member of *La Compagnia delle Poete*, a theatrical Italian co-operative of poets.

Sally Read is based in Santa Marinella, Rome, and in Bungay, Suffolk. She is currently poet in residence of the Hermitage of the Three Holy Hierarchs.

SALLY READ

THE DAY HOSPITAL

A POEM FOR TWELVE VOICES

BLOODAXE BOOKS

ISBN: 978 1 85224 948 9

First published 2012 by
Bloodaxe Books Ltd,
Highgreen,
Tarset,
Northumberland NE48 1RP.

www.bloodaxebooks.com
For further information about Bloodaxe titles
please visit our website or write to
the above address for a catalogue.

Supported by
**ARTS COUNCIL
ENGLAND**

Cover design: Neil Astley & Pamela Robertson-Pearce.

Printed in Great Britain by
Bell & Bain Limited, Glasgow, Scotland.

For Kerry Lee Crabbe

ACKNOWLEDGEMENTS

Acknowledgements are due to the editors of the following, in which some of these poems first appeared: *Sally Read reading from her poems* (The Poetry Archive, 2010), *The Manhattan Review* and *Southword*.

Thanks to Gregory Leadbetter, Roddy Lumsden and Baron Wormser for their continuing support; to Agnes Macioł and Tom Grubb for checking the Polish lines; to Asceterium Sanctorum Trium Hierarcharum for helping me to face the larger questions; and to Fabio and Celia for giving me the time to ponder them.

CAST

All patients of The Day Hospital for the Elderly in Central London

8am, NW1

Traffic is gridlocked at Parkway, Camden High Street junction. Rats run over empty pizza stands. Voices, footsteps are lost to the rising wash of traffic. Smell: weed, rotten cabbage, cold stone, exhaust.

Bodies streaming out of the tube are propelled by likely shunts from behind, probable collisions, noise, the precise calculus of minute by building by minute, by the woman with grey wool hair and shopping trolley at 8.05am:

'Death! Destruction! Despair!'

Words are gunned down by cars. A giant blue rocking chair is nailed to a wall high above the street. A giant boot. A bluebottle. Ranks of pedestrians wait at a curb; lean in to the cars; almost fall; fall at the green man – Go.

Theresa stands at a bus stop, passing a carrier bag from hand to hand.

Pat sips coffee in the Day Hospital lounge.

Agnieszka wakes in her penthouse flat, thinks: This is the day.

A 75 year old Irish man with a history of depression. A frontal lobotomy was performed in 1955. The reasons for the operation are unclear.

Pat

What I did I don't know
A voice asks me

I push a heap of tobacco to a line on thin paper
whistle the round
and complete Danny Boy
to its end
to its dog-end and past the end of breath
and its end

What was it they asked me

I live alone
with bed, table, chair
a worker comes in
to help with the tea
and the dressing

In the handful of grey stuff
they took
they took the know-how
of buttons, trousers
the front-backness
of a shirt

the what-order of kettle, tea-bag
water, cup

They took the wit
to assemble
the old know-how
of mixing sand, water
cement
of trowelling the gritty wet
not thin or thick
of laying brick
after brick
after brick
after brick
after brick

Rain blinded me
and my fingers
it gulped off my cap
as I squinted down
This is life, I think
thrown hard
and pouring off you
as you do your damnedest
to look away
to not be blinded

while you wait
to do the pointing

make the smooth seam
between the balanced
bricks
check with the bubble
of spirit-level
that it won't slouch

Was it a chair I threw
in some hospital ward

A long way from home
no money
the restless city
a bellyful of anger
that they took out the brain

Was there a girl
they asked me

There was not

There was chips in paper
a rented room
a single bed
a gloom like a gloved hand
leant on my chest

I was quick to fists, yes
the orange beer-light

the fug
the rattle of cash
the stone jeering
of men
and I wanted the punch
for the dead cold to come up
warm, red
alive

Was it a chair that I threw

It is not
that I don't remember
but that the pictures
come sideways
at once
and won't come through the mouth

It was a long time gone
fifty years

The bed
the kettle
the social in jeans

They watch me
as I watch the thin white paper
the neat line of tobacco
They watch me

the young doctors
and I hum
Danny Boy

This morning
they point out a picture
a complicated
tangled thing
with no order
too many people
a light
shadows

people
too many people
short and long
a light at the centre
and much dark

They ask what I see

I finish my song
I breathe
I whistle it again

I see a moon
I say
a moon outside a window

A 65 year old devoutly religious Irish woman with a history of schizophrenia.

Theresa

On your knees in the Church of Our Lady,
tuned to the turning of your own mind,
and in its spaces hearing the empty sea shell
that can be God
                              it is hard to separate the voices.
I told Charlie I thought there'd be more fields.
Where was the green: my whole vision,
all my life green – where'd they put it?
and he laughed so hard he hit me.
Charlie wasn't expecting fields. He expected
cranes and building sites and cash in hand.
7am, the Church of Our Lady, there is no one
but me and Father John, and a down and out
who sleeps in the church porch.
Vespers, sometimes a choir, and two or three
regular ladies, all Irish, plus the occasional
youngster who sits through it like the cinema,
or Japanese tourists coming in late
with their umbrellas and paraphernalia.
Would you stop looking at me like a frightened rabbit?
Charlie belted as I came in
which made me open my mouth like a fish
and earned a slap. What in God's name, he'd say
as he lurched out the door.

Our life, our sweetness, our hope
Poor banished children of Eve.

It was after the death of ma they got worse.
The call came to the pub two doors down,
and the barmaid came knocking at 9pm
shivering, skittish, in her short-sleeved sweater
and me so conscious of troubling the girl
and the bother of it for Charlie it didn't occur
to me to feel sorry. Not even when,
come the morning of the funeral in Bantry,
I was in Our Lady in Camden,
trying to pray but instead going over the ferry fare,
and the bus fare from Cork to Bantry.
Hail Mary full of grace, the Lord is with thee.
The statue of Our Lady was smooth enamel
and haloed with small electric stars. Poor ma,
I prayed, and then asked forgiveness for not
being more careful with the money.
And they came in blinding flashes
like someone else's fireworks.
Eat shit and die! Feck the lot of yez,
cock-sucking bastards...
No!
My mouth had the air and taste of it,
but there was no echo from the stone,
and the down-and-out slept on in the back.

I go to bed fully clothed and don't undress,
even to wash. The leap of my own skin
shames me. Charlie upped and got a job
elsewhere. In the sick-light of dawn
I see him going home. I clean the church
and also the rectory. I collect money
in Oxford Street and take meals
to the sick and the old. The house empty
like I could make it green – no carpet, no TV,
no books, all those corners for grit, dust,
sin and slime. I holler a prayer in my head
and dig my nails in my palms so they bleed.

Only sometimes, standing in the stream
of bodies on Oxford Street, watching them poor
foreigners with the sandwich-boards and banners,
only sometimes I think the soles of my feet give,
as though they couldn't sense the ground –
like your hands do when you think you left
your purse on the bus. I think of home
and ma and da. Charlie when we first wed,
the roads I walked to school and church. I lost
my footing. Somewhere I lost that weight
a person feels to keep them married to a road.
My feet twitch and know the air, as if I flew.
And then I think of all those eyes that watch you
coming at you up the street, and without
knowing you sum you up to nothing,
or strip you down without a word.

And I know if I went back home there'd be
no place for me. Or if there was my eyes
would be so full of all this, so full
of all this

I sweat, white, I shake the flesh, oh shame
to leak such water from a body I can't get clean
I scour my hands, I scrub the presses, try
to keep the enamel statuettes in my head,
my gut, all stood up straight like nine-pins –
Mary, Joseph, John the Baptist, Cecilia
decapitated, Catherine starved purer than fire –
but they shake, the roar within me toppling
them – *Fuck yez all, Pack of wankers* –
toppling the most whole, the most pure
who sang even as they was slaughtered.
The Church of Our Lady, I pray the Rosary every day,
fifteen decades they say, a day,
they say the devil is kept at bay, they say
you will not be left in misfortune, they say
you will be comforted in death, they say
a place for you awaits in heaven, I say
the Rosary and it is like one white feather
among a maunder of bulls, like wind
grabs the words from my mouth
which I stuff with small beads of pills
and finger the rosary, finger, finger
and even this is unclean, cleanse me Father
I have sinned, they say the clean will enter

the Kingdom of Heaven and she is there
on the right hand of the Lord, Our Lady
with no hands, no sex, no shame

They give me pills in a box-contraption now
so they can see my cheating. I bicycle
to the hospital and sit with nice ladies
in a group. The voices are silent for days
then they come, quieter than before, but
clear, and the young nurse stares at me
like she can hear them too. You'd
want to die, God forgive me. Routine,
they tell me,
                Fill your Hours with Doings.
Father John likes his presses scrubbed
with the carbolic, and his shirts starched
daily, and his tea with hot milk, and suds
to be rinsed off plates with cold water,
and his cabbage mashed with Colmans,
and his bed turned down, and new shoes
bought from Russell and Bromley,
and mirrors polished to spotlessness,
and the TV wiped with a special cloth,
and corners vacuumed with a long attachment.
So my hours are strung and even there
the darkness collects like muck.
When I enter the sacristy he does not look up.
Like a brother, like a husband, like a father.

A 68 year old Polish Jewish woman with Alzheimer's disease who arrived in England with her mother and brother during the Second World War.

Agnieszka

Name? Agnes.
How old are you? Oh.
Do you know what day it is? (pause) Thursday?
And the year? Oh. Nineteen. Eighteen. Oh. *(laughs)*
And the prime minister? (silence)

Why these questions?
If they had asked about a broken plate
on a red floor
I could have told it.

A red floor.
Sitting cross-legged
with a menorah in my hands.
It wouldn't fit into the case
and I thought I would have to carry it
a very long way.
I was ten.
          How old are you, Agnes?
I know the question. My mind
slips up and down years,
unable to stick (Am I young or old?
Am I married? Do I have children?)
It's walking through a familiar room,

but the furniture is smothered in sheets.
White space where words
should be,
the tongue a thrashing muscle
hooked to nothing.

My mother never sat down.
Her wild effort
kept me and Tomas standing too.
Father, she said, was still in Poland.

Agnes, we're worried about you getting lost.
I walked out of my flat in my white
cotton nightgown with blue forget-me-nots
embroidered on the collar, and crept
barefoot down Roslyn Hill.
A nice girl brought me home.

Mamo!

Mamo! Dokąd poszłaś?

Benny Best was a restaurateur
with ideas above him and everyone else.
He took black cabs to Oxford Street,
sat in Lyon's Coffee Houses
swilling tea and taking notes.
He was all show: silk waistcoat,
trilby, stumpy cigar, glasses,
an adolescent haze of beard. His smell
of smoke and Wood's kept me

the other side of the table.
I thought if I put my hand out
it would go right through him.
But no kvetch, Benny Best;
and a sense of constant motion.
So I married him.

                 Sometimes,
when I set out Shabbat dinner
in Hampstead, London I feel
my stomach glitch. A part of me
in Warsaw, a good chunk
in the East End.

                 Now I am escaping him.
I disappear from the bedroom,
into the mirrored lift. I slide
from the dining table into the hall closet.
I roll under the high walnut bed.

Odejdź ode mnie. Potrafię rozpoznać

Nazistę.

                 In my home-town,
my normal Warsaw, odd twists
like a dislocation of bone –
the picture-house out of bounds,
mother's blue and white china
smashed on the floor, girls
from Pani Lenski's class throwing

stones at me on the way home
from school. I stood so straight and tall.
My stockings came down around my ankles,
but I didn't stop and pick them up.
I was sorriest for that.
Then Muriel Maier said one freezing
London afternoon, Your dad is dead,
and she said it like an accusation
of stupidity. No, I said, without
looking up from my blue marble.
I knelt my bare knee on the pavement's
slime, rolled the marble straight,
and got the whole and answering
clack.

Morning's blurred clarity.
So many leaves.
You could hide in this tall morning,
in London's high deep pockets.

> *Have her hatted, coated,*
> *bag packed, by 9.*
The Filipina answers
the door. I am hatted, coated.
A brown leather bag packed.
Everything answered in one bag.
A person, a bag.
I would unpack it, hurl each thing
as far from the other as I could – toothbrush

in a flowerpot, nightdress in the freezer,
documents flushed in the toilet bowl.
I fear the scattered drops of me
collecting, coming
together, they come
to collect me
            Agnes? I'm from the hospital.
Shall we go downstairs?

This is how they come. Not with guns.
Not with kicks at the door. A knock,
an exchange of glances, they come
to collect a woman, a packed bag.

The doctor, she says, *the doctor will speak*
to you, come, come and Benny will come
and if you don't want to stay you can leave.
You're a German aren't you? Well I won't go,

no, thank you. I tear open the bag, chuck
books, nightdress at them, grab the knife
(I knew to pack a knife). I rip my dress, push
it off. I climb to the window, raise the knife.

I bang glass with a shoulder but it won't smash.
There is crying, the dark maid is crying,
(so this I smashed), the German is standing back.
Touch me and I jump.

I scratch at glass so fast it is gentle
and see blue and white plates
whole and in pieces: an oriental temple,
delicate trees. Then, in one sudden shard

a tiny blue boat I had never noticed,
a man at the helm, pushing himself
downstream. That picture, so accomplished,
I almost put it in my pocket.

Come up, bring the Haldol.

They march in behind me, one each side,
each take a wrist, each take an elbow,
and lift me, so – clenched – I fly.
They tip me down to my knees, bow

me to the floor, my cheek pressed
to the sudden fibres of a rug.
My arms pinioned behind me, my head
gripped between two black knees.

The skin and shape of my nose
is crushed. I smell cigarettes,
wet leaves. Someone pulls down
my underwear. My eyes pressed.

My mind a wisp. Someone draws
the sign of the cross on my buttock,
and then scrunched muscle's lanced,
a thuggish throb's released, bludgeons

through the cowering blood. Becomes
bigger, bigger till it circles me:
the brace of bone at my skull garners
fear, movement, words. Collects me.

No room. No room. No room to be.
Only to hear. A song above my head.
Someone whispering my name.
Mamo? To ja, Agnieszka.

Agnes, can you tell me where you are?

10am, NW1

Traffic roars. Fits the head like a balaclava. Cars mass, flash grey light. Only screams and shouts are audible as individual voices. Sirens, at their most intense pitch, reach top-floor flats.

Flats: pockets of heat and silence. The white sky is too big for the window. Hiss of sofa foam. Waiting.

Grit articulates itself under the sole of an approaching shoe.

The lift smells of day-old piss.

Trundle, trundle, grind, goes the lift.

Zigzag patter goes a shriek.

Maurice is at home, waiting to be dressed.

Jack is at home, waiting.

Bridget is at home.

Barbara waits for answer.

A 74 year old Jamaican who emigrated to London in the 1950s.
Diagnosis is still uncertain.

Maurice

You think I don't know the room smells of piss?
Even the light's urine-yellow
and them thick curtains pissing out
the natural thin light of London.
Even the carpet's loaded with it. Even
the thin thin pages of these books, floppy
with heat and piss.

                   Look, I can hardly
walk. Whoever thought of putting a toilet
all the way over there?

                   Don't hurry me.
Let me show you my history books.
Chapters on Empire, sun never setting –
I like that. British do OK poetry.
That red sun's filtering through me piss-
soaked curtains right now.

                   What I need's
a woman. God's last laugh: the only
woman sees me naked comes to soap
me poor ole back. I drop the soap,
goad her to rummage between
me legs. She laughs like a tea-spoon
in a china cup. Can't tell if I's kidding.
Neither can I.

27

She's white, mind, like all
the rest. White like da light, white like da law
white like da music and da talk. I
no time for white women. Since
1951 I have Susan, Abigail, Serena,
Jane, Maureen, and Molly. All white
but Molly. All cut and run. All teetering
about on heels and taking taxis to offices
and the drivers won't pick us up,
and the neighbours put dog dirt through
the door. Molly cut too – died of cancer.
Blew in from roughly my part of
the world, and there's no not telling
a black woman between the sheets.
They know the timing, the tick
tick tick, like they sit on the wrist-watch
of the earth, like it's calibrated
to the blood.

         When someone's gone
you spend your days with your hands
heavy, held out heavy in front of you
with what you didn't give them.
Molly wanted a child. Six children
to be exact. She left six brothers
in Kingston, and come to clean up
after hundreds of whites in Holloway Road.
She pass me every morning as I clean
wheelchairs in the sluice, and my line:
I got da rush in my feet still.

We thought we was so damn lucky,
scraping shit out the seams of a chair.

                         Months later,
kissed and sniffed, and fucked and
danced and talked out and heard
and tired, she says to me: I don't want
no more rush. I don't even wanna
go home. I want roots, and roots
isn't back, roots is down right
where you're standing.
She mean she want to plant children.
A forest of children. Then
she'd live in her own world,
the rightest person in the rightest place.

                            London.
You got your Pakistanis and your
Bangladeshis, your Ghanaians
and your Indians, your Turks
and your Italians, your Poles
and your Portuguese, all glitter,
glitter and odd-shaped vegetables and
spices and things taste the same, almost,
as home, but tell ya what, after fifty years
who knows what home tastes like.
All weaving they little forests under
the wedge of grey sky, sits on your brow
like a sledgehammer.

                       Up and down the wards.
Some the nurses thought they was so

classy flirting with a coloured. All them
straight-down girl in blue with they
rod-gait, streaking down corridors.
Up and down with sick folks and old
folks and stiffs wrapped up in sheets.
Every month, old Molly with her mop
frowns a groove deeper, sways her hips
a shade heavier as she hustles that mop.
Ten years mop-hustling, no kids.

                              Then, pregnant.
And she walks Archway like she's carrying
a world. Like she barely owns that round pelvis,
like if she sneeze it falls off.

                                  I spend my life
in hospitals. Hospitals is like some
intact galaxy. You get born in them,
you work in them, you occupational
terapize in them, you sick in them,
you die in them. You don' need
leave the place at all.

                                How many nights
I spend blowing wages with Ronny Scott
and Jack D and when I look back
or hear the ring at the door it feels like
I barely leave the hospital lobby.

                                Help me into me
trousers. I know I shake like the Acropolis
if the Acropolis was about to fall.
Lemme sit. Pass the Rizlas.

Take a look at the next book
in the history of the world: the Twentieth
Century – gone so fast the bits flown off
still twirlin'. It's how I see her,
her and that lost baby, clamped together,
whirlin' – no roots, no home
(see, I don't include the plaque
in the crem garden) – but one complete world,
twirlin'.

And then I'm on the day hospital
bus, packed with Jews and Irish and Poles,
Betty with her knickers round her ankles
and John lurched forward like he died
already. *Keep movin'.* The young nurse
springs on like a baby mountain goat.
Git goin' and I shake me stick high,
and have 'em all duck. *Don' keep me waitin'.*
Speed man. It's the only way ya don' fall off.

An 80 year old Londoner with Alzheimer's disease.

Jack

Blue sky! Lovely out.
Here's tea, chivvying in its saucer.
Plash, tink tink tink of tea.
No birds. No birds. Blue sky.
Lovely out. Whassya name?
Whassya name? Whassyname?

Wife

Would you know the shape of thought
without words?

Would you know what presses in the throat,
and stern of head
has taste of coal or earth or sex or metal
presses backs of eyes?

No birds. No sounds in the brain
that join and cradle and make
a circuit snap.
Parts that don't conjoin.
Cogs, pistons
come apart.

Then –
        memory:
              metal worked with lathe.
White sparks, white heat. Once,
for a minute, I left the goggles off,
woke that night and couldn't see,
the film of vision scorched,
memory of blindness,
paralysed
in a jagged black room:
arc-eye.

Then: memory, burnt off.
Clean. Like grease under hot water.
Like baked fish-skin
puckered,
shrugged off. Pass the salt!
I say, pass the salt! What's ya name?

How quick a man's mind
picked clean.
                Down the dock.
Down the dock. Down the dock.
Clank. Fast-moving feathers, smell of mud
and fish, crack of ice, pint of bitter,
a hot black window.

Nothing sticks.

I wake, blind.
I open my mouth, silence.
I hear, rubbish.
Rubbish rubbish rubbish

Then, a flash! Bob's your uncle:
Maureen, more tea!
Nailed it.

There's something at the core, the rough
breadth of chest, like blood, like cables,
snakes eighty years.
This is all I know when knowing is no more.
When there are no badges
to tell who or where
or how long.
Only a thing without a face
without an age
and
words charred to black
and come apart.

What sticks?

She ambles in with tea-cups,
a way of leaning on a hip,
Where's the baby? I say, where's she put the baby?

How quick a bloke goes.

No talk of soul.

Nothing whole.

Chemicals firing

a picture, a word;

dying.

A 76 year old Irish woman with depression and agoraphobia. She has not left her flat for two years.

Bridget

It's years now I wear
the old flat like a coat,
its pockets stuffed
with screwed receipts.
The neck reeking
with the wearing of it.
You all come in
with your pills and soaps.
But this is living.
Everything outside will come in

Even on that grey way
to the lift I feel my innards
disappear and the air
gone through me.
It's like it sifts
and spreads me thin,
butter on toast,
and my heart gives in –
melted butter.
The unlocked door
is jammed with post
Even in my hat and coat
I look like I just got off

the toilet and left
my bedroom slippers on.
Everything outside will come in

The light of the television set
washes through me
like a nip of Jameson's.
The nip of Jameson's washes
through me like a man's
five o'clock shadow on my cheek.
The man's shadow goes through me
like a cold walk in winter fields.
The fields go through me
like a Sunday roast.
The taste buds drench me
like dead kisses, resurrected.
The dead kisses sit in me
like old potatoes stinking
double with their own lost life.
The unlocked door is jammed with post
Everything outside will come in

I used to cry that John didn't speak.
Now I cry because I miss
the deaf-ear, the smell of Vicks
and football on the telly.
I cry for the ironing I took in:
'I can't,' I'd say, 'I can't, let me sit down,'
and maybe I did, but got myself up

like it's a call from God,
and smoothed it through
and sat again and if the chair
wasn't there you would carry on
falling and not move
as you fell.
Everything outside will come in

Ashley's gone. Got herself
a coloured and went to America.
Her father's gone. *Gone to the air*
would spread me thin
Everything outside will come in

Doctor says this is no life.
He's wrong. At night my heart's
the loudest thing in this blasted flat.
It beats and laughs like a kid
with a torch hid under a quilt.
My neck creaks like a door,
my guts squelch out a symphony.
My soul trails sorely over every
fibre on the floor.
The unlocked door is jammed with post
I live like I was hanging on
to a horse throwed me off years ago.
My hairs are on end with it, this living.
Everything outside will come in

A distressed 69 year old Londoner. Diagnosis still uncertain.

Barbara

Dizzy? Nah. Nauseous? Nah. Scared? Nah. Sad? Nah. A white for the 'eadaches, a blue for the 'pression a yellow for the blood pressure. Can't descrive it. Wish I could. I come over all queer. Queer? Lost me senses in Londis. Fell on me bum on the bus. Wake in the night shouting Where am I? Where am I? 'You're in bed, you moo,' 'e says. It's the flat: so high. Can't see the tree tops. Can't hear the birds sing. 'What's you want,' 'e says, 'an aviary? Move to the zoo.'

Children never came, Sister. Do I mind? Yes and no. I stacked shelves. Did I like it? Yes and no. I liked getting out. We forget to get out, don't we Wilf? Sometimes it's dark and I says, We got no toilet paper love, get down to Londis, and he does, but it's too late. There's the hamsters, gotta be fed and watered and cleaned. What are their names? No names, Sister. What else? The doctor's for prescriptions. The clinic. The social. We got the occupational therapist coming Thursday.

We're not like them Greeks upstairs, Sister, always carousing. Hot-blooded. We got no telly, no hi-fi, no bookshelves, no armchairs, no candles, no papers, no flowers. 'Candles? Paper? Waffor?' 'e says, What if I wanna write something down? I says. 'Like what?' 'e says, 'You can't write, you mare.' I could draw, I says. 'Draw what?' 'e says. A cat I says. 'For what?' 'e says. Dunno.

Too dry for sad. Too still for fear. Too much in me head for sick. Worse at night when the Greeks are a-bed. And I think to meself The whole world's in bed. The whole world's gone dark. I float. Can't stay on the bed. If 'e lit a fag, it'd be something to look at. Don't want a picture. Don't know what a picture is. Wouldn't know how to look at it. Can't read a book, don't know how to try. All them little black lines, thousands of 'em on one page. Exhausting. Nothing touched. Nothing ever took. They put me on the till once. Didn't like it.

Nothing touches. 'E hasn't touched me in years. Do I care? Yes and no. No use crying over spilt milk. Stiff lip. Chest out. That's what me ma always said. Too dry for sad. Too still for fear. Yes and no, yes and no.

There is something – nights – come to think of it. Foxes shagging their guts out. Hear 'em all the way up here. Thought it was the devil, first time. Thought it was a kid ripped to bits. 'Just a fox,' 'e says, 'getting off.' I wait for it some nights. Do I like it? That devil-sound? Fills a hole. When all's too quiet. Fills a hole. All quiet. Too high for birds. Nothing above us. White sky. Nothing else, sister. All done and dusted. Nothing else. Table laid and done.

What?

What pills Sister? What does the doc prescrive?

3pm, W1

Rain. A bass beats through a shut car-window. Shops beat music. Shoppers weave Oxford Street, slalom into Greek Street. Steam from alleys. Side streets are empty. Nude shows in six-foot red letters. Daylight on the veined, pink rubber dildos. Red nylon and crotch-lacerating red lace. Berwick Street Market still has a flower stall: 'I used to sell flowers there. Me ma did too. Tulips she liked. Pink'uns.' Fresh buns, organic leeks, Agent Provocateur. Blue ostrich feathers and turquoise fishnets. 'A real village, innit? Sense of community.' A low red sports car cruises Old Compton Street, hurling condoms at passers-by. St Pats is open: Romanesque arches and incense in open darkness. Above sex-shops, in peppercorn-rent flats and felt hats, sit Daphne, Eva, Millicent, shaken every so often from their thinking by a slide of red neon across the floor.

Across two streets the Day Hospital windows are blank.

Anna is being led to a piano.

Catherine has come back with a bouquet of pink roses.

An 80 year old German Jewish woman with a history of schizophrenia, suicidal ideation and self-harm. She emigrated to London in her early twenties, leaving her mother alone in Nazi Germany.

Anna

(Kriah – the rending of clothes in grief)

The new clothes must be broken.
I pick at one stitch
till a chink admits a hole,
then blackens till it bleeds.
Cuffs are worried to a fray.
The new shoes must be broken,
interrogated at the mouth
till the black skin splits.
An old woman in rags,
I do not speak.
Hunched over a frame,
head bowed as though
endlessly pushed down
by some higher hand,
my silence is a labour –
I rock, pant, I shoulder
quiet like a boulder, let slip
gasps, wheezes, spit.
I do not leak a word.

The nurse is still and thin
as blue milk –
it disturbs, her stillness.

She weighs me, weekly.
Pinches the skin
on the back of my hand,
observes its slow un-tenting,
and sits opposite me
as I guard my mouth.

Forty weeks I do not speak.
The silence, I suppose,
a package to be undone,
round as skin, packed dense
as gelatinous intestines –
I keep all balls in the air
I keep the thoughts from settling
I keep the shots in barrels
I keep the January crows
from cracking open
like champagne
I keep taxis waiting
and sirens looping
I keep the drunken street-
fight a white second
from its first punch
I keep blood from letting
I keep questions from being
answered and the sun from
weakly darkening, I rock
and tear and rip the buttons
from my shirt

Let me show you something:

a photo on the nightstand:

my mother walking with a girlfriend
in a Berlin street
seventy years ago. One hand
at her skirt,
the other on her hat
that threatens to fly off.
A stopped laugh.

Mutter
Soldiers cried it in the trenches.
A child will cry it even
to her own mother who she hates
at that moment
as a comb is yanked through
tangled plaits. As though
there is another mother,
always, a lost mother,
the godhead voice
amplified through skin,
a dark sea,
and then the tap of milk.
The woman in tortoise-shell glasses
and an odour of overcooked cake
is flawed. Soft brown
sweaters and stuffy scent,

her voice fuzzing through her chest
to my pressed ear.
I hadn't cried it in years
but when the letters from Berlin
stopped, when the telegram
came, and I still walked to work along
Belgrave Road, past grey shops and
black absences, smell of burnt
wood and kerosene I would feel
the word in my body as I imagine
a woman feels her unborn child.
When I sat at my desk,
muting my German voice,
I thought it would escape,
a foetus in the shape of a word –
Mutter

The nurse sees my face is broken
by a choir of voices:
Jump   Slash   Die
They instruct me.
They are so real in the room of my skull
I fear they can be heard.

Naked women dragged
by their ankles like slaughtered calves
Socket-eyes   Shootings   Rapes
Starvation   A tangle of glasses
and shoes   What tiny civilisations

they had to step from
to give themselves
as raw
dissolvable forms

I have a new skirt.
The stitches at my knee tease open,
a trembling pleasure –
like peeling sunburnt skin.
What are you afraid of?
The thin, white nurse asks.

death and judgement
cutting of engines
missed trains
the shipping news at night
new clothes
the settling of bills

The blouse is white, the hems so hard
to pick you'd need a toothpick
worry, worry
till the cotton gives up its groomed
thread, and furs
Let me show you
the flying space between two neat
and settled
stitches

how it exists
how it does exist

Now, I suspect if this nurse had cracked me
if I had begun to tell

the story would be long gone
hardly begun
and me stone-dry
stamped like a fossil
the tenacious curve of history
pulling me into this shape
Ich kann nicht sprechen

I am in the first flush of grief
the panic and the jubilation
Shiva has not passed
(it drives the years)
the smoke has not stitched itself
into the blue air, the heart's
charge keeps
the mind warm
the eyes burn
and cannot focus
I dread the first night
the final listening
though I am here, in a London hospital
in nineteen ninety-eight

Anna, would you
play for me?
On the pock-marked hospital carpet
in the curtains of congealed smoke,
the nurse guides me
to a piano.
I place my fingers over the keys
and sense anticipation.
The boned keys arch to meet me
soft as bone,
as soft as bone, alchemised,
can become –
like a woman's belly
the sigh of a young woman's belly –
that yielding.
But the notes, that pure
and whole song, Mozart's
exacting engineering,
I can't provoke it
or spike the air; I will not speak
I will not deliver
a mother's life,
have her
so sonorously
undone.

*A 70 year old Irish woman recently recovered from depression follow-
ing the death of her husband.*

Catherine

Nurse, would you tell me when you marry?
I will make something fine –
a veil, a shawl, a babby's bonnet.
I could needlepoint God Bless This House.

When you look into the eyes
of your first born: think of me.

I am the Faith gets up at six to sit in the church,
hear the day break outside. As though night
sealed up roads, doorways, scars and they're unpicked –
fresh, unhealed – by the light. It starts

with the stir of a tea-spoon. Cars tearing
quiet to pieces. Sirens jumping. I deadhead
brown chrysanthemums, messy tongues of lilies.
I sweep the floor, polish the chalices,

lay out the vestments. And still there is an hour.
So I sit and look at Christ in the dome.
The eyes that follow you around a room.
I look at Him and He looks at me.

I offer my stillness in the city that's shifted
like a cold stone to set free its ants. Sometimes
my neck plays merry hell, my eyes ache,
but I look and feel the lines around me break

and not a clever prayer in my head. *Love,*
love, I whisper, and think of my babies –
now grown girls driving to offices – and how
I was never alone when they were in me,

when they were months out of me.
But there was always a time, a night,
you'd lie next to them and feel them go –
hard, separate in their dreams. Grown out

of the fluttering pods would snooze at your side.
Is that the soul its own man? Finally free
of its mammy? Then the loneliness would find me
as though I lay on a beach and the cold sea

crawled to me on its belly like a snake.
And I would come here and look at Him
and ask, *Love, love.* And receive only blackness
in the asking eye. Only blackness in all my hollows.

Only a nourishing blackness. Until the day
the Unlit marched in. The Unlit, I call it.
Not the dark of presses, wells, and eyes, or the silences
that call an echo. The Unlit is the winded black

of a cut-out paper woman. Make me small and flat,
I seemed to say; give the pain less place to dance.
But the pain was in the flatness.
I feel that folding in my throat now.

Shane was dead and gone. I never reckoned:
how much he propped me in my loneliness.
And as I sat in the church the face of Jesus
hardened to paint. I looked at the world;

it did not look back.
                    I do not dwell.
I am come here to say thank you for the Faith.
For the words, the pills, the groups, our talks,
but above all the words. I could have taken them

home on their own, and set them on the mantle
and looked at them, and known of their working
like the cold, un-rested waking of the city.
Words which opened me up again

to the rich and empty spaces –
You will be well. I've seen your kind before.

5pm, N1

Dusk, puddles. Traffic gathers constantly; a giant reshuffling of intentions. Windows along Torrington Way come yellow: a woman pulling a cake from an oven, a man watching TV, kids colouring at a table. From one window, a smell of burnt sugar floods the road.

On Holloway Road a pub is open. No music. Floorboards creak under the barmaid's shoes. The pub sign swings and complains.

'Save me, save me I just want to die.' 'You leave the room I kill myself.' 'Save me. I see myself hanging from the apple tree in the garden; look out the window, there I am.' 'Talk to me five more minutes.' 'Can I call you at home'? 'It's all right for you. All right.'

The city saves its moments: rooms without music; sporadic silences; conversations in hospital rooms or cars; sex in upstairs rooms, or deep in alleyways. The illusion of privacy in a space narrow as a vein.

Daniele is standing.

Ruth is cycling.

Tatiana is sure.

A 65 year old Italian Jewish man who arrived in London during the war without his parents, stands on the roof of a 14-storey building.

Daniele

Birds sing up here, for no one. Above trees. Higher than God's domes in grubby dusk. Birds sing. Indrawn breath, but no time, no brown field for surprise to settle on. I am the highest point. Eye drawn down, sucked down. Almost sucks me off this roof. Tremble. Below: black Victorian hospital; grit; water in the air. I stand, ready. No. The opposite. Breath short. Heart eking out its round of blood, like a breathless, impatient, hungry mother. I am unready; it is time.

Dogged steps to get here. Dogged. Stop at red man, go with green. Goad the sea of blunt men and women squinting into blank white sun. Crisp packet caught in my gait. Dogged. On and on. No brown field to let breath rise up from. Breath, breath. Comes short. Blue, grey, creeps at fingernails. The day is ending; I can't put the lamps on! I've rushed around a dusky house punching switches. Tired! A man in brown cashmere coat who sold insurance, had season tickets for Lords, clasped a woman's ears as he fell into her. No. No. No. He yelled. Thought: too much. Trouble. Birds sing up here as if none of it happened.

Mother stood with me at the Arno's edge

Walked, walked, walked Highgate Hill, Archway, buoyed on the city's womb-hiss. Twice stopped in life: once at railings cut with blossom. Sat on curb in grey suit. Could walk. No longer. Once could not roll myself from bed. For mother? For father? No. Enough. Tongue pawing its final mouthful. Heart stomping dust. Guts farted out and flat-packed. Enough.

> *Mother stood with me at the Arno's edge,*
> *Nazis coming, water a softer death.*

Birds sing up here. Little scalpels of dusk-sound. Victorian hospital black with wet. Deadland around it. Beyond it chug and screams of Holloway Road. So much wet it clings to skin. On ground: glass in shivers. An upturned wheelchair.

> *Mother stood with me at the Arno's edge,*
> *Nazis coming, water a softer death.*
> *She stood, considered, my hand in hers*

Down, down below, nurses in blue jump from a bus. No brown field to settle on. Dio, Dio, che fai?

> *Mother stood with me at the Arno's edge,*
> *Nazis coming, water a softer death.*
> *She stood, considered, my hand in hers,*
> *made a basket, stuck with pitch and prayers,*
> *pushed me to England, far from sight.*
> *I stepped from a train to infinite light.*

Which is not to say; which is not to say. Eyes cased in film, heart ready to break its shell. Dissolve of blue nurses into building below me. What is outside is over. I bend my knees.

Fall

Flip ten windows; six nurses see for one half-second. Thick growth of adrenalin. Blood a cilia of hooks to cling to cling to cling to anything. Crackle of water pouring down arms cheeks: adrenalin. The mind: **No**. Flips cards, photos; synapses fire. Alight in a millisecond on a hot narrow road, open trap filled with tomatoes, cloud of flies rocking with the stink. Following that trap. Following that trap. Following that trap. From nowhere, from under the lining of memory. What images the mind throws up – firing, clicking, chucking up.

Explosion. The world explodes. Not just me. Everything shaken by some great bomb. Hot wet black bathes my eyes. The world explodes. I explode. The world in my mouth, fit between bridge and tongue, the world inside me blows me open. Or dissolves in me. So that is it; all this cut-off is the end and the answer is the end. The end the answer. An answer will only be an ending. And the rattle-gummed, maladetto, shattered skull gargles its last epiphany – holds it aloft in rampant triumph: this is it! Quiet. Blinking, in breathless quiet of truth. Red, heightened red. Brain slurping great truth with its last sense. Light white light. Now a clearing. It's OK, I can almost stand! Now I see, a clearing. Black. Black. Not sound, deeper. Not sight, deeper. Deepest. No memory or germ of life.

What I do not see: the police tape around my thrown body. Slashed sandbags. Sand to soak the blood that moves without me; the urgent endless blood. Look what moves without me.

Ruth

Where was God in Auschwitz?
Where is God in this hospital?

Where is God? The nurses sip tea, play
music, and try not to laugh. They're young;
I try not to laugh with them.
My backhand suffers, my eyes strain to read,
my knee aches as I cycle.

Yes, I will cycle, all 80 years of me; feel the ache
of the synovial joint; push the pedal through
and round it.
Know the shaft of pain along the shin;
pedal past it (see how it falls off, the pain,
in the patter of spokes).
It might be time to give up the bike! The physio simpers
as we exercise in our chairs, stretch, bend,
dance in our chairs, march, wave, debate
and love and hate and fret and die in our chairs.

Where is God? Solly moans, and kicks
from his wheelchair. All the poor Holocaust
orphans, now more wizened and old
than their parents ever became:

Rebecca who learnt English from Pope,
Harry whose tongue stalled from grief,
David who mimics Hitler and starts
the daily jousting of canes.

I'll tell you, wise girl, down to the hidden corner,
the shards of broken matzo on the floor:

God is in the concentration camp
guard's footstep;
the will to follow; in the mass shower
and suffocation;

in the noose made of sheets;
the yellow, strangled face.

In unstirred tea, and Betty's moans
as she eases her sores from the chair.
In the smell of shit and old flesh;
the stash of untaken pills up Margaret's sleeve.

In the guard's footfall to murder,
there is a vacuum and there is God's vigil.

He crouches like a birthing woman
trusting the head to crown.

He labours, like a gardener,
in the small-work of cells, the splitting
and embedding.

He prays, like one of us, because
in that dark night prayers
are a murmured exchange
with Him.

We drowse over unstirred tea and mark
yells from the dementia ward.
Where is God? Solly moans.

Shalom little brother, I want to say, but can't,
and mount my bicycle and free-wheel
the Deus ex machina of pills in my pocket

out of city streets, into the darkening park,
pushing that strangulated knee-cap
undoing its resistance,
and using each girded
muscle to light and flicker, and warm.

A lack, an absence, is also a want;
a want a quantity to be filled.

What fills, wise girl, is another agent, apart from us,
yet in us (in our tongues, minds, and hearts)
incarnate from the impossibility
of absence.

The guard's footfall would murder God;
it begins the impossible, never accomplished task.

My father's death in life, my mother's
death in life, my aunt's death in life, my
grandmother's death in life. I pedal
Autumnal air, so cold it judders and burns.

London is fields, black trees,
wind to cough a person out
of her skin. The trick is to twist each cell
with and against it, to jostle and refract.

This is Grace, in death, in love;
the old losses turning, kept alive
to glean unto the end of barley harvest...

This is Grace: God blushing in me, as I fly,
like a recently eaten meal.

A 90 year old writer with vascular dementia who emigrated from
Russia as a small child with her parents.

Tatiana

Listen, a married man in the hand
is nothing till he's – ha! In the bush.
You know. Isn't every man married –
married to something not you? I knew
the odds and the score – empty nursery,
tall evenings of sleep and books
and the gold, red icons cooking my wall.
Look dear: mottled eyes, mottled hair,
mottled chairs. Old age is a grief
of lost edges. Pens all bled out,
roofs that don't spark, threads not waiting,
all what's-the-word, all gone.
Listen – a Russian choir, fifty years past.
It's, what's the word, – clouds, fog.
I see the moon and the moon sees me.
Did I hold the key? Did I think there'd be hell
to pay? Stuff to lay? Every life has a lack.
Look at the icon. I'm not Russian.
Mother and father. This music, this icon.
Put it in your pocket as you go.
Past windows, yellow indigoes,
every one a still-life: some woman,
cooking, waiting. Every city is married
to someone not you.

Don't tell them about the glove on my foot
or the back-to-front dress.
Dressing on winter mornings is fingers
and thumbs. Numb tangles of socks, legs.
But not the end of – end of – end of –
end of –

      I'll stay in my own house, own rugs
to trip on, own clothes to sit backwards in,
own music for memory, my cashmere
gone grease-stained, my icons burning
the walls. It is a long way home to be
buried.

      There was one. There was one.
Who made the lack I sit with my back to,
travelling backwards. That lack, pushing us on….
 – I kissed him once, the kiss so long
and hard and still we nicked the –
the tiny skin anchors the tongue.
He fucked me, and I moaned with a voice
I never heard again: no voice but sound
drawn up past words, houses, rings,
chickens, blessings and brides.
Did you ever hold all the cards in your hands?
Did you have a ring on every finger and thumb?
Did birds chatter on your shoulders and knee?
Was the way through the wild wood free?
Were there whispers of promise and blossom, blossom?
Was the white church within earshot
And blessings rung out before dinner was done?

Sound: like a beast heard across the night.

Cards flew to the ground – no sound, no sound.
I was thingummy – I watched them,
white birds that didn't know how to let
themselves fall. I held all the whassanames,
wreathed, sheathed, peeved – and I know it now
The answer to all
the saving and scavenging and catching at light
that covers the hole, the hole, the hole,
as it smallens
I have the answer now.
Let me see...
If I could just remember
the word –

NOTES

Catherine

I look at Him and *He looks at me* were words spoken by a French peasant to Saint Jean Marie Vianney. The saint, then a parish priest, had asked what the man was saying to Jesus during the long periods he spent sitting before the altar.

Ruth

To glean unto the end of barley harvest is from the Old Testament, Ruth 2:23.